My Disappearing Steps

COREY THOMPSON

MY DISAPPEARING STEPS

Copyright © 2024 Corey Thompson

All rights reserved.

ISBN: 9798304562782

DEDICATION

This book is dedicated to all my fans, friends, and family who stood with me and prayed for me in my jungle. I had specific family members who were there from my initial sermon, when I began as a pastor, when I started my church, when I left the church, when I began my health teaching, at the birth of the Pivot Up organization, and that helped me with various events. To all of you, I want to say thank you.

People counted me out, talked about me, and left me, but God kept me while I was on this journey. If you stayed with me in prayer or with positive words, thank you. Many of you witnessed my spiritual and career growth and supported me as I ascended this ladder of success. My social media support was astonishing. The consistent love, comments, and shares on my motivational videos were mind-blowing. The consistent speaking engagements from various cities, states, and platforms are becoming transcendent. All I can say is this book is dedicated to you and anyone whose life is positively impacted by the words printed on these pages.

TABLE OF CONTENTS

Dedication
Acknowledgments

Introduction 6

The Calling 11

The Jungle Entrance 14

Egypt/Kemetic 19

Voodoo 22

Satan Worship 24

Atheist 26

Conspiracy Theorists 29

My Return 30

Fiery Exodus 33

Who or What is God? 35

My Motivational Journey 36

The Knock of Death 38

The Takeaway 42

Goal Setting 44

My Quotes 50

About the Author 51

ACKNOWLEDGMENTS

I would like to acknowledge Dr. DeAngela L. Haynes from Encourage97 LLC for taking my vision and turning it into a masterpiece. Her impeccable skills, hard work, and positive words through the process of bringing this book to life are remarkable. If you desire to publish a book, I highly recommend her services. She is a one-stop shop for any upcoming authors. She is also spiritual, anointed, and ready to serve the needs of authors. Self-publishing becomes a lightweight when you have someone who will steer you through the process. From the bottom of my heart, thank you, Dr. Haynes. Your irreproachable skills will help millions through the life of this book and every book you publish.

INTRODUCTION

Have you ever wanted anything so badly that when you got it, it changed your life forever? Now that I have extra blood flowing to your brain, hold that question. Are you taking life for granted? Life is a precious gift that was given to us. Having a life is not a curse, but the decisions we make create hard times. I get it, we make decisions based on the opportunities we have before us.

We don't intentionally travel the road of poor choices, but that road leads to the ditch of regrets. Have you heard that hindsight is 20/20? To have 20/20 vision means that you can see perfectly without eyeglasses. Hindsight is 20/20 because when you look back on your decisions, you can see the bad choices you have made.

The best ways to make better decisions are to sleep on it, pray or meditate about it, have a trusted friend, or enter into it with your eyes wide open. So many of us make decisions with our emotions and not with our conscience. I call this an emotional selection. These are a few tools that won't rob your joy from life. We need to continue to enjoy this one life that we are given and stop taking attributes of life for granted. These encouraging words I had been missing for some time. I was on top of life and living a good version of life, but what I once knew as a good life had disappeared. What was once familiar quickly became unfamiliar.

Your current life, you know it. You know where you work, where you worship, what you drive, and so on. If you are walking from a place, you know your steps to return, and you know your steps ahead to your destination. What do you do when you stop recognizing your steps or the life you once knew? This happened to me. It wasn't a concussion, amnesia, or any other mental disorder.

My steps I once knew disappeared, and I stopped recognizing life. I felt like I started journeying through the jungle of life. Before my steps disappeared, I had a promising and successful path in ministry.

Before my ministry commenced, as a young man, my parents kept me in church. Seemly, we were at church more than home. Church wasn't a boring place because my brother and cousins kept it alive in our ways. As a youth, I was also active in church. I was one of the lead singers in our young men's choir. Keep in mind, I wasn't blessed with a voice that knows how to carry a tune, but that didn't stop me. In my mind, I was being brave for the Lord.

Some of the first songs I learned were, *Come along my friends* (Ride this train) the Canton Spirituals version, *Anyhow* by Tommy Ellsion, and *He Got the Whole World in His Hands*, just to name a few. I was asked, "Why does it sound like you are talking when you sing?" The voice wasn't present, but the passion was. You may not have the talent to do certain things, but your passion could cause you to shine brighter than talent.

My parents did all the right things, such as praying as a family, teaching us to pray every night and morning, having in-home Bible study, and teaching us about God. They did not spare the rod either. My opinion at that time was that their chastisement was too harsh and cruel, but now, I see that as a broken muscle. For a muscle to grow bigger and better, you have to rip the muscle through some type of repetitive resistance. Their chastisement broke me and made me a better and stronger man.

As I entered into preteen, the seeds that my parents planted began to take root. My spiritual life was beginning to sprout and blossom. I received salvation at the age of twelve, and I was baptized by thirteen. I started carrying around a little red Bible that only comprises the New Testament. I challenged myself to read a chapter every night. I did and completed the entire New Testament over time. When I entered my teen years, I got involved with teaching Sunday School and leading devotion at my home church, Mt. Herman Baptist Church.

My faith started growing tremendously, and I began to pack the scriptures deeply in my mind. I have had several family members come to me and ask me what the Bible says on various subjects. I was becoming one with the scriptures. When you become one with your desires or passion, you funnel your future with peace and prosperity.

As a preteen, I started spiritually strong. Around the age

of seventeen, I allowed peer pressure and the spirit of curiosity to take over. I began to live and experience the other side of this spiritual life I once knew. However, even though I journeyed away from my spiritual roots, I was still tied to the ground that my roots were in.

After experiencing the other side of my spiritual life, I was drawn back to my roots. For years as a youth, different people saw a huge calling over my life. My pastor, at that time, told my parents, "That boy is going to be a preacher." I found out years later that he told my parents that. Sometimes others will see our destiny because our journey could be clouding our sight.

THE CALLING

In October 2003, I received my calling to preach. One Saturday night, while asleep, a hand appeared out of the clouds along with the roof of a house. This hand had a hammer in it. As the hammer hit the last nail on the roof, I heard a loud and deep voice that said, "PREACH!" When I woke up, it felt like my soul was on a trampoline. It was an unforgettable and uncontrollable feeling. I ran to my parents and said, "I think I was called to preach."

My mom said, "You can't THINK, son; you got to know." I then said, "I KNOW I was called to preach." Sometimes in life, when you know what you know, nobody can take that away from you. My knowing was confirmed by my leaping spirit, my dream, my desire, and through the spiritual lens of others.

When I shared this experience with my pastor, he just smiled and nodded his head. He knew before I told him. Keep in mind, at this point I was so excited and eager to preach my initial sermon. My pastor quickly threw water on my flaming ambitions. He said, "I am going to take you through a year of training before you preach your initial sermon." I was thinking to myself, "A YEAR!" Today, I am extremely happy that he did, and it paid off. Don't be afraid to sit on your passions, dreams, or calling for some time. That period will condition you for what's ahead.

After my year of training, I was able to preach my first sermon on October 17th, 2004. The title of that sermonic presentation was, "How long will you falter between two opinions, who or what will it be?" I came from 1 Kings 18:21. According to the response of the audience, preachers, and my spirit, it was a success.

Two years after my initial sermon, I was hired as a pastor at another local church. The membership and the finances grew rapidly. Unfortunately, unforeseen circumstances pushed me to resign less than two years later. During this period of time, I was averaging 10 to 15 preaching engagements a month. After I resigned, I had around thirty-plus people who traveled with me as I preached in various places. Success and blessings were chasing me during this period of time.

With the amount of people who followed me, I was convinced to start my own church, so I did. In 2008, Abundance Grace Outreach Ministry was born. Because I was the founder of this ministry, I had free rein to follow my God-given vision without having a board to approve it. Abundance Grace was a successful outreach ministry. But then, in 2010, one question that popped into my spirit would change my life forever. This question was the beginning of my steps disappearing.

THE JUNGLE ENTRANCE

I had no idea that I was about to enter into a spiritual jungle. The steps I once knew were about to disappear before my eyes. The success I gained over the years was about to be flushed away. The question that led to a quest that altered the trajectory of my life forever was, "Why do we worship on Sunday and not Saturday?" I went into an in-depth and extensive study on this subject. While I was studying this subject for months, I can remember praying to God and asking him to give me a clear answer.

Apparently, God was ignoring my request. I can remember secretly getting frustrated and a little upset with God. "Why don't you just make it easy and tell me?" "You see, I am trying to do the right thing; please show me the right way." I was questioning God almost daily. I am so glad God didn't give me the answer directly. The reason why I am happy now is because that question took me on a journey that taught me a lot.

After I got over my frustration and anger with God, I wanted to know, "Who is God?" While on the journey seeking answers on the original day of worship, I made another deal with myself. I said I wanted to know this true God for myself.

At that time, I knew God through the teachings of my parents and my pastors. "What if they were taught wrong?" was a question that came to mind. For me to know God for myself and to introduce God to humanity, I became naked. I went into a really deep study seeking so many answers. Everything I was taught growing up as a Christian, I decided to research. The more I researched, the deeper I got into the jungle.

During this time, I was still pastoring a Christian church. I feel as if one of the biggest mistakes I made was as I was learning the truth behind man-made holidays and other information, I was teaching it to the church at the same time. It was a mistake because it was like feeding a baby a whole cow. The church was not prepared, conditioned, or spiritually mature enough to handle the multitude of information I was throwing at them. Even though I was becoming convoluted, the members and ministry remained intact because this was a church I founded. After a few months, I exercised my God-given wisdom and stepped away from the members and ministry. I initially stepped away for a year. I allowed other preachers to come and preach in my absence. During this year, I got more involved with my studies. My studying led me into what I now call "the spiritual jungle".

My first stop in the jungle was becoming a Messianic Hebrew. Messianic Hebrews believed in Jesus and the New Testament. As a Messianic, I started worshiping on Saturday; I altered my diet according to the Old Testament diet, I allowed my beard to grow out, I kept the biblical holy days instead of holidays, I wore fringes or tassels on my garments, and so much more.

I started studying under a rabbi and got involved with that understanding. I started learning the Hebrew language to better understand the scriptures before the Greek and English translations of our current Bible. Eventually, I became one of the teachers of the Messianic group I was a part of. As a Messianic Hebrew, I was not content. I kept studying to see if there was more, and there was more.

As I kept studying, findings in the Old Testament writing made me question the New Testament's validity. I dived deeper into the Old Testament, and I started questioning who Jesus was. As you can see, life is about to take me on a swift and sharp turn. As I journeyed deeper into this jungle, because of my studies, I journeyed away from the belief in Jesus and the New Testament. At this point, I only believed in and lived by the Old Testament. During this time, I considered myself a Hebrew Israelite. I was no longer part of the Messianic group that I congregated with. This transition lasted a few years. As a so-called Hebrew Israelite, I was not content. I kept studying to see if there was more, and there was more.

I started studying Muslim beliefs but never became one. I realized that Jesus is mentioned in the Holy Quran. His name is translated as "Isa ibn Maryam," which means Jesus, son of Mary.

The Quran also references him as "al-Masih," which means Messiah.

According to scholars, Muslims can be traced back to Ishmael, the son of Abraham. Scholars teach that Genesis 16-21, shows us the beginning of the Muslim understanding. If you consider yourself an Israelite or a follower of Jesus, then Muslims are your spiritual brothers and sisters, and we all share the same spiritual father, which is Abraham. However, I was not content in studying Muslims. I kept studying to see if there was more, and there was more.

EGYPT/KEMETIC
Herbs/Health

Because I kept studying, I entered into the study of ancient Egypt, aka Kemet. As I journeyed into the Kemetic understanding, I was losing my grip as an Israelite. I dived deep into the deities of ancient Egypt, such as Ra "the sun god," Osiris, "Haru," Isis, "Aset," and Horus, and the list goes on. While I was studying ancient Egypt, I came across a man named Imhotep. Imhotep was a genius in his time. Even though he had many attributes, the one I gravitated towards was his herbal and health knowledge. Because of him, I became very inquisitive about the human body and how to heal it naturally.

I started studying and using different herbs. Because my knowledge of herbs and illness grew immensely, I started studying and teaching health classes. At one point, I was making my own medicine from herbs. I became very guarded about what foods I allowed to enter my body because I wanted to be as healthy as possible. My quest to be healthy took me from 250 lbs to 187 lbs in a matter of weeks.

So along with learning about ancient Egypt, I learned a lot about the function of the human body and healing it. I also learned a lot about Africa as a whole and how it was the birthplace of humanity. While studying a lot of the ancient civilizations of Africa, I realized that God is bigger than just one religion or denomination. Also, many ancient African beliefs believed that God was a woman and not a man.

It has been taught that men stripped women of their power to be leaders or goddesses for their selfish gain. Even though men have minimized women, they are still powerful creatures. Even currently, a woman has power over a man's mind through various subconscious manipulations and their childbearing ability.

Women should be respected more around the world because life comes through them. This leads me to my next question: Did we shrink God to a gender? If the Divine Energy that created everything shows up now and it is not a specific gender, would you recognize it?

It's funny how we squeeze the creator of everything into our small box in life. We war with others based on our beliefs. Our beliefs have chopped God on the cutting board of our misunderstanding and blended God in the blender of confusion.

Even though I felt that I was at the root of understanding God, I wasn't content. I kept studying to see if there was more, and there was more.

VOODOO

As I was navigating through Africa's belief system, I came across what we know as Voodoo/Hoodoo. In studying Voodoo, I realized Hollywood and other mainstream media have demonized Voodoo.

I got extremely involved in Voodoo because it reminded me of Christianity. Let me explain before you stop reading. Voodoo is a monotheistic understanding, which is the belief in one God. They also believe in Loa. Loa are spirits; some refer to ancestors. It is taught that ancestors are around in the spiritual world protecting us. The belief in ancestors, Lola/spirits, isn't strange in the Bible.

According to the Holy Bible, it is recorded in all four gospels that Jesus' transfiguration was witnessed by some of his disciples. (Matthew 17:1-8) During this mountain experience, their ancestors, Moses and Elijah, appeared. This is only one of many examples that came from the Bible that display the presence of or belief in ancestors/Loa that isn't taboo or wrong. Well, what about other things in Voodoo, such as the root doctor, black magic, and spells?

Well, let's talk about it because I went deep into this as well. I began studying with and under voodoo priests. I learned the art behind casting spells and debunking spells. Allow me to warn you, black magic or spells should NOT be attempted by anyone who doesn't know anything about it because it could be very dangerous. Spells and black magic are only wrong and evil when they land in the wrong hands.

They use the power of manipulation to make something go in a certain direction. Many of us use the power of manipulation or mind control to make things go how we want them to go. We should learn the power of influence instead of control. There is nothing wrong with manipulating some using the vehicle of influence to positively alter the trajectory of their decisions.

MY DISAPPEARING STEPS

Root doctor! I was also seen as a root doctor because I was into herbs. A root doctor uses herbs and other things to make different potions for healing and other spiritual things. Jesus spit on the ground in John 9:6 and made mud to heal a man's eyes. Some natural minerals in certain dirt could be medicinal. Because of this, you can view certain dirt as herbal. Even though being a root doctor has gained a negative name, if it is used correctly, there aren't many differences between them and a pharmacist or your local physician.

Voodoo, magic, and the root doctor aren't all bad. The hands that are carrying these are dirty. Because of that, we see them as wrong or dirty. If you are being led by the spirit, don't be afraid to study beyond what you have been taught. For me, I kept studying to see if there was more, and there was more.

SATAN WORSHIP

As my studies continued, I came across Satan worshiping. Yes, what you are thinking now is true. I got involved in invoking the devil and evilness. At this point, seemingly I am out of control. Little did I know, God kept a leash on me while I was on this wild journey.

I started viewing Satan as the one who opened humanity's eyes to the truth. According to the book of Genesis, it was the devil that tricked Adam and Eve by eating from the Tree of Knowledge. Because of this, their eyes were opened to good and evil.

I also started learning evil rituals, and I was allowing the devil to take residence in my soul. Even though I was beginning to esteem evil, I was not content. I kept studying to see if there was more, and there was more.

ATHEIST

After exploring other small religions and belief systems, I realized the majority of them were man-made. Because they were man-made, the rules and regulations that came along with that belief system were the opinions and feelings of the man who made it. Houston, we have a problem! If they are man-made and I was able to trace the man that made them, what about my belief?

Am I now living according to the rules of man and calling it God's path? Am I minimizing my desires in the name of man? Am I praying to a god that was created by someone's brain? Is my conviction that I am feeling when I do certain things linked to my traditional teaching of man and not God?

One of my objectives when starting this journey was to get to know God personally instead of through the teachings of my teachers. I wanted to introduce to the world the real God and not the god that was made up through someone's imagination. But now, the words that are reverberating within me are, "Does a God really exist, or have we been tricked?"

Around this time, I was developing an agnostic belief. Agnostic believers believe that either God exists but will always be unknowable or God exists and he/she is just sitting back without mingling into human affairs.

My views of life then took a sharp turn. "There isn't any god." I officially became what we know as an atheist. Wow! From a successful pastor to now an atheist. Around this time, I developed a hatred for Christians and their traditions. I began to mock them and some to their face. I started living without boundaries. I started drinking and hanging out in places I should not have been, I got involved with psychedelic drugs, and I untamed my tongue and allowed all words to rip.

One night, I wanted to see how drunk I could have gotten. I decided to mix brown and white liquor, and I kept drinking. Needless to say, I got drunk. My mom grew very concerned about the choices I was making. My dad went to my previous pastor to express his concerns about my new life. I was getting reckless with my life.

This whole journey started with me wanting a closer connection with God, but now I am down a dark, deep, scary, and lonely hole. Be careful how you stroke your curiosity, because some journeys are non-returnable. When you allow the spirit of curiosity or the spirit of peer pressure to visit you, be ready because it will try to take over your residence. Please keep some doors closed. Because once they are open, for some, the only door that will close is the door of their casket. However, even as an atheist, I was not content. I kept studying to see if there was more, and there was more.

CONSPIRACY THEORISTS

During this time, I became a conspiracy theorist. I also studied heavily on the Flat Earth theory, Nibiru (a planet that has life and giant creatures), and Chemtrails (the cloud of condensation that comes from planes). I used to believe this cloud had chemicals in it to control humans, shape-shifters, fake suns, aliens, giants, black holes, the new world order, sleep traveling, portals, Sumerian understanding, the all-seeing eye, space, and the list goes on. As you can see, I studied almost everything. However, I was not content. I kept studying to see if there was more, and there was more.

MY RETURN

While I was journeying through the jungle, there was a pastor from Detroit, MI, named Dr. Tellis Chapman, whom I kept listening to. Even as an atheist, I was drawn to his teaching. I feel as if God used Dr. Chapman's teaching to keep me from disappearing completely. I also had the prayers of loved ones that served as a life vest so I didn't drown in the water of investigation.

Because of this, the fire of preaching was ignited again. My love for teaching never died. I went to my dad at the beginning of 2019 and told him I was feeling a pullback into the ministry. After my crazy journey through the jungle, I wasn't sure how to return. My dad said, "Son, if you are ready to come back, then God will make a way for you to return."

A few months went by, and my dad was still encouraging me. He was my number one fan in the ministry. As I was pondering how I was going to return, my dad passed away. I wanted my number one fan to witness my return. While we were planning his funeral, my siblings and I called an older cousin of his to eulogize him. My amazing aunts entered into my head saying that I should do the eulogies. They said, "You know he was your number one fan." I gave in and listened to them.

Two days before the service, I had to call and explain to the pastor who was going to eulogize him that I needed to do this. That pastor said, "I knew you were going to call." He understood completely and said, "I will be there to support you." I preached at my dad's funeral, and officially I was back. Churches started calling me again to do what I love, that is speak. Life is getting back on track.

All of the information I learned on my jungle journey, I was able to bring it with me to help others. The Apostle Paul said in 1 Corinthians 9:22, *I have become all things to all men that I might by all means save some.* At this point, I felt the same way. Because I became so much in eight years, I feel as if I can reach almost anyone while being spiritually led. However, I was not content. I kept studying to see if there was more, and there was more.

FIERY EXODUS

Were you born of a woman? The obvious answer is yes. With that being said, we all experience some type of fiery situation throughout life. As the Bible stated in the book of Job, a man that is born of a woman is of a few days but is full of trouble. We usher some of our troubles in because of our choices. Because I chose to entertain the approaching journey into this jungle, I ushered in fuel for the fire of despair. We know that fire can burn up or clean up things.

Even though I gained a lot on this journey, I also lost a lot. My fiery furnace burned off people I was connected to, negatively affected my relationship, burned off the life I once knew, and much more. It cleaned up my narrow view of life, my misteaching of religions, my understanding of God, my understanding of life as a whole, and much more.

Do you have what it takes to allow your fire to turn into pure gold? You already know that you will experience trouble in life, but I dare you to allow your trouble to mold you into a masterpiece. Why go through the fire without having gold to show for it? I thank God for my fire because of my gold. My gold from my fire is an increase in knowledge of life, health, spirituality, and other historical things that were washed by deceiving humans.

You must have a plan of action and an end goal for the fire that you may enter. If you are in a seemingly unending battle with life, try something different. Also, be careful how you re-enter into a fire you have been delivered from. So many of us are polished like gold, but we head back to a situation because of familiarity. Always allow the spirit to lead you because you could be directed back into the fire to finish developing into gold. Because God has delivered me from my fiery situation, I am now polished for my purpose.

WHO OR WHAT IS GOD?

God is... that's it, God is everything. Every organic creation has a piece of God. This divine energy created the motion of every atom. If you understand the organic form of nature, you can understand God. When you spend quality time with the higher version of yourself, you are spending quality time with God. When you gain control of your emotions, actions, and thoughts, you are on the road to discovering the higher version of yourself. Know yourself to know God.

I am not calling you a God, but I am saying that God lives within you. God sits on the throne of our higher conscience. If I have to speak scientifically, God sits on the throne of our pineal gland. Stop allowing people to define their God to you, and get a relationship with God. Seek God, and God will find you.

MY MOTIVATIONAL JOURNEY

The fact that I came back should have been the end of my story. I went from a successful pastor to an atheist and back to a believer. However, as I stood on the stage of churches, delivering my sermonic presentation, I felt restricted. The majority of the churches are packed with people who believe in Jesus. Let me make this clear: there is nothing wrong with being a believer.

However, as big as this world is, not all believe in Jesus or go to a church. Some people hold fast to their beliefs and are ready to die for them, just like Christians. A lot of traditional churches cater strictly to the older crowd, which does not leave a lot of room for the youth. Both churchgoers and non-churchgoers experience trouble.

Both churchgoers and non-churchgoers need help in various forms. In other words, regardless of a person's religion, denomination, age, race, gender, and lifestyle choices, they are still humans who need help from time to time. So I was not content preaching and reaching Christians only. I saw a hurting human race. I saw people who could benefit from a motivational word and other tools. Being led by the Spirit, I decided to extend my reach to schools, the streets, prisons, various camps, and so much more. I became a motivational speaker and a trained holistic health coach. I wanted to reach Christians, Hebrews, Muslims, agnostics, atheists, or anyone with their hands extended for help.

I felt like the Apostle Paul, in 1 Corinthians 9:22. God allowed me to take this journey so I can reach and inspire all people. My steps disappeared before my eyes because I didn't recognize life anymore. I later learned that my steps did disappear. The reason my steps disappeared was because God was carrying me the whole time while I was journeying in the jungle of life.

THE KNOCK OF DEATH

Throughout our lives, death will knock on our door. The knock of death could come in various forms. Death knocked on my door several times throughout my life, but a few specific times my journey through the jungle kept me alive. "God kept you alive, Corey, not your jungle experience." Wait, let me explain.

My father and grandfather died in their late 50s from heart issues. All my life, I have masked my heart issues from the public. When I was young, I visited several heart specialists for my heart issues. In my mid to late teen years, I stopped experiencing issues with my heart. In my late 20s and 30s, I became a workaholic.

There was a period in those years when I started averaging three hours of sleep during the weekdays because of my dedication to providing a better life for my family. My average day during a period looks like this: I wake up early in the morning, get ready for work, and then drive 30 minutes to work. Once I got to work, I spent between 30 to 45 minutes getting my paperwork for my route, getting my equipment together for my workday, finding my tractor, and then logging in. I would work 14 to 16 hours on the clock some weeks.

As soon as I got back to the terminal after being on the clock between 14 to 16 hours, I logged off immediately because as a truck driver, we couldn't work any more than 14 to 16 hours a week. After I logged off, I had to fuel my truck, offload anything that was left on my trailer, and turn in all paperwork. So, once I logged off, I spent another 20 to 30 minutes at work before driving 30 minutes home. Once I got home, I got my clothes and food together for the next day, took a shower, and handled any small business that couldn't wait.

I only had about three to four hours left some days before my workday started. Because of working like this for years, I was beginning to wake up to my heart issues. In my mid to late 30s, my heart issues returned. I was under a lot of stress during this period which made things worse. I started dealing with major depression and anxiety. My depression was so bad, that I gave a family member all of my passwords to everything because I was convinced that tomorrow may not come. Even though I tried to hide my depression, it was beginning to show because it was so severe. I tried to suffer in silence, but by doing that, I was taking years off my life.

Please stop suffering in silence and find a trusted person to talk to. A simple talk could add years to your life. "Corey, how did your journey through the jungle save your life?" Well, one night while standing in the kitchen, my heart gave out. All I remember is a sharp pain in my chest that had radiated down my arm. My breath got very shallow, and I became weak. My head was spinning, and I temporarily lost control of my body.

I am a strong-minded person with a powerful will and untouchable determination. I also have a very high tolerance level for pain. That night, my heart temporarily got the best of me. After composing myself, I got up and eased into bed. Throughout the next morning, I was weak, in pain, and felt nauseous. My family begged me to go to the doctor, but I was too stubborn. About a week later, I wasn't feeling my best, but I was on the road to healing. I started pulling out all the knowledge that I gained over the years to treat myself.

I finally went to the doctor about a week and a half later to see if my heart suffered any damage. The test results showed a little scarring, but for the most part, I was good. Even though I don't know everything about the human body, my exposure to knowledge while I was in my jungle helped me to remain alive. Yes, my jungle experience kept me alive this long. When death knocked on my door, I answered it with faith, prayer, and the knowledge that God granted me.

THE TAKEAWAY

I have studied many belief systems, and all the major ones are pointing at one thing: you being the best version of yourself. When you can tap into your greatness, you will foster love, peace, and happiness in your life. The best version of you is on the inside of you. We have to become detectives of our soul, to extract what God has impregnated us with.

The best version of who we are, is bound by our purpose. We have to spend quality time with God and ourselves to know our "whys". Imagine with me, there is a long line of souls in heaven. Each soul was given a bag by God. In a roaring voice, God said to each soul, "Everything you need to survive on earth is inside this bag. Your peace, love, happiness, purpose, health, wealth, and a key to your blessings."

The problem is, we are so busy operating out of someone else's bag that we don't open ours. We are too busy trying to be like the next person instead of being who God wants us to be or created us to be. What's in your bag? Are you living out of your bag? Do you know how to open your bag? The bottom line, we all should subscribe to the best version of ourselves. We war over beliefs, religions, and other diminutive things. This needs to stop! Let us learn how to make ourselves better and how to operate using our higher conscience.

Let us learn how to respect other religions and beliefs and stop expecting people to think like us. Let us continue to look at the soul of humans because most of us are pure at the soul. Stop thinking negatively about people and learn how to assume positive intent. Remember that your future self is counting on you.

GOAL SETTING

When I started this journey, I had an end goal in mind. Setting goals for yourself is essential for success in your next chapter. Setting goals is the destination. You don't learn anything by setting a goal or reaching your destination. The lesson is always learned on the journey to reaching your goals.

Keep in mind that my end goal was to get to know God and to bring God to the people. I felt as if the God we knew was damaged by mankind. I had no idea when I started this quest that I would have ended up getting involved with so many religions or other belief systems. As you can see, this journey has taught me a lot.

What goals are you setting for yourself? Remember, once you have set your goal, get ready for the process or the journey. Allow your journey to build you, mold you, and condition you for your destiny. Because I allowed my journey to mold me and condition me, I am now able to speak on almost any stage to any crowd. The reward of not giving up on the journey outweighs the obstacles I had to endure. What is your goal? Is it to lose weight, make more money, heal your relationships with others, become a better person, find a better job, go back to school, complete school, and the list goes on?

Once you have set your goal, you now need to make it up in your mind that giving up won't be an option. If you learn how to become one with the process, it will make it extremely hard to give up. What do I mean by becoming one? When I left the church, I became a full Hebrew Israelite. I changed what I wore, what I ate, and what I did. I also learned how to speak Hebrew. I had fringes at the end of my garment, and I grew out my beard. I started studying with rabbis and other Hebrew scholars. In other words, I became one with that.

When I started learning about ancient Africa and started studying a man by the name of Imhotep, I started applying his herbal teachings. I started taking herbs, selling herbs, and making medicine strictly from herbs. I also taught herbal classes. Some of my herbs were imported from Africa or other countries. I bought a book by a herbal doctor, and I learned how to mix the right herbs. You see, I became one with that knowledge. When I started studying space, I bought a telescope and other devices that helped me track planets.

I was able to see the color rings on Jupiter and the ring around Saturn. I enjoy staring at the craters on the moon and other planets we hear about but can't see with the naked eye. Once again, as you can see, I became one with my studies. Whatever goal you set, try to become one with it by buying what you need to buy, studying under experts, and thinking about it often.

When you become one with your mission, your YouTube playlist should be full of that particular subject. Once you have become one and have studied all around that subject or that goal, start teaching it by creating videos or teaching small groups. When you teach it or create small videos, it helps you retain it more, and people start looking to you as an expert on that matter. As they look at you, they will come to you with questions. For me, if I did not know the answer to a particular question, I would go and study it. As I studied, I gained more knowledge on that subject. With Google, YouTube, books, and other experts, it is easy for you to become an expert in a particular subject. Do not research one thing and start teaching but research your research.

The bottom line, get married to your mission. You have been dating your purpose or mission for a long time; it is time for you to get married to it. For me, I am married to my God-given mission. Because I am married to it, besides God and my family, it is my number one "WHY" I'm here on earth. This means that if you're not for me or my mission, you are automatically against it. We cannot allow anybody to cause us to divorce our passion, purpose, or goals.

So once again, what is your goal or desire? Do you desire to open up a business, start an organization, or write a book? Do you know what it takes to accomplish that goal? Are you ready to do what it takes to accomplish that goal? Are you ready to give up your free time and place most of your energy towards that goal? The only person that is stopping you from reaching your goal is yourself. So many of us think that it takes money to start whatever we desire to do. It takes a made-up mind, and you dedicate yourself to it. I heard Les Brown say, "Impact drives income." Become an expert in your journey and try to impact people. The Bible says your gift will make room for you.

Once you have set your goals, studied all around it, and are ready to move forward, get with someone who is already moving. I knew I wanted to be a motivational speaker, so I started connecting with other motivational speakers who could accentuate my gift. Because of pride, so many people are afraid to ask for help from someone who's moving in the direction that we placed our goal. The fear of reaching out equates to the complacency of staying put.

When you don't step forward, you automatically step backward. The world we live in is constantly moving forward. In order to keep up with the world, you must bury fear and resurrect faith. Now is the time. Now is your time. Don't let another moment pass you by without you setting your desired goal. Continue to pray and keep God first. Use your God-given gift to make your life better. Remember, everything you need is inside of your bag of life. Reach in your bag and go be great. Stop just being alive and live.

I pray that this book gives you the fuel you need to become all you can be and to be the best version of yourself.

MY QUOTES

I live by many quotes that I came up with. These quotes are:

- *"Allow your push to be greater than your pull."*
  Make sure you have the right people in your life that are pushing you.

- *"Let your present be right for your future, so your past won't haunt you."*
  Today is your present. When today leaves, today becomes your past and tomorrow becomes your future. Make the right decisions today, for tomorrow. The seeds you plant today will be for your harvest tomorrow.

- *"Put do before doubt, never put doubt before try."*
  Keep believing in yourself and your God-given abilities.

- *"Learn how to press to leave an impression so people can press in pressure towards their purpose."*
- *"Stop trying to control the waves of life and learn how to ride them."*

- *"Staying down is a decision of refusing to get up."*

- *"A good towel could become an old rag if you use it too much."*

  Be careful how you allow people to use you!

- *"Forgiveness is a medicine that heals the heart."*

- *"Don't doubt in the dark what God has shown you in the light."*

ABOUT THE AUTHOR

Corey Thompson a native of Manning, S.C. He is the second-eldest of four, and the son of the late Deacon Ulysses and Retha Thompson of Manning, SC.

Corey is also a renowned traveling motivational speaker and a trained holistic health coach, with a career spanning over two decades. In 2003, he was called to preach, and he preached his initial sermon in 2004. He became a senior pastor in 2006.

Corey's passion lies in assisting individuals in discovering their purpose or "why," providing them with a focal point as they navigate through life. He believes that understanding one's purpose is essential for personal growth and fulfillment.

Corey's holistic approach encompasses physical wellness, mental clarity, and spiritual alignment, aiming to foster a balanced and healthy lifestyle. My philosophy is that words are life and energy. I love to impart these powerful words into the souls of humanity, inspiring and empowering others to reach their full potential.

As a motivational speaker, he has had the privilege of addressing diverse audiences on a multitude of platforms, covering a wide array of subjects. His extensive knowledge and experience allow him to connect with people from all walks of life, meeting them where they are and inspiring them to reach their full potential. While his top topics include purpose, health, life, and goal-setting, he is versatile and adept at engaging audiences on any given subject.

Corey has been privileged to receive many awards and accolades throughout my career. He's had the esteemed privilege of receiving my honorary doctor's degree in divinity. He has also been featured in several magazines highlighting my philanthropy contributions.

Corey is also the founder of Pivot Up. Pivot-Up is a non-profit organization that concentrates on the restoration of the mind, body, and soul through various services and methods.

Made in the USA
Middletown, DE
06 March 2025